ALFRED'S DRUM SHOP Series

HOW TO TUNE YOUR DRUMS

the most complete reference guide available

Dave Black

Cover photo courtesy of Remo, Inc.
Photos on page 4 courtesy of Yamaha Corp. of America.
All other interior photos © Alfred Publishing Co., Inc.

Alfred Publishing Co., Inc.
16320 Roscoe Blvd., Suite 100
P.O. Box 10003
Van Nuys, CA 91410-0003
alfred.com

Copyright © MMII by Alfred Publishing Co., Inc.
All rights reserved.   Printed in USA.
ISBN-10: 0-7390-2454-X
ISBN-13: 978-0-7390-2454-6

CONTENTS

Introduction 3
Drumhead Selection 3
Obtaining the Correct Drum Sound 3
The Drum and Its Parts 4
Tuning the Drums 6
The Snare Drum 7
    Changing the Drumhead 7
    Tuning the Snare Drum Using
        the Cross-Tension System 8
    Tuning the Snare Drum Using
        the Clockwise System 10
    Setting the Head 12
    Using the Snare Adjustment Screw 12
The Bass Drum 13
    Changing the Drumhead 14
    Tuning the Bass Drum
        (Cross-Tension System) 15
    Setting the Head 16
The Tom-Toms 17
    Changing the Drumhead 17
    Tuning the Tom-Toms
        (Cross-Tension System) 19
    Tuning Multiple Toms 20
    Setting the Head 20
Muffling 21
    Muffling the Snare Drum 21
    Muffling the Tom-Toms 21
    Muffling the Bass Drum 22

Special thanks to: Dave Tull, Rod Harbour, Dave White, Kate Westin, Kim Kasabian, Steve Harder, Link Harnsberger, Bruce Goldes, Yamaha Corp. of America and Guitar Center.

INTRODUCTION

How to Tune Your Drums is a well-organized reference guide for drum students, professionals and educators alike. Written in an easy-to-use, step-by-step format that includes lots of photographs and diagrams, this one-stop sourcebook covers everything you need to know to effectively and consistently tune your drumset. It covers topics including drumhead selection, changing a drumhead, tuning your drums, and important concepts such as muffling and obtaining the correct drum sound. As with any book, the explanations do not attempt to cover all drums or tuning possibilities. Readers are encouraged to experiment on their own, as such creativity is essential to finding out what works best.

The following material is presented in an interesting and satisfying manner, ensuring you'll find this resource guide helpful in your pursuit of musical excellence.

DRUMHEAD SELECTION

The majority of today's drumheads are made of plastic or other synthetic material. Batter heads vary in thickness (thin, medium and thick) and may be either transparent or opaque. Though not affected by humidity, plastic heads can be affected by temperature, making them brittle during cold weather.

Calfskin heads, which were once used for all drums, remain available but are no longer popular due to price and maintenance factors. When used, they are more appropriate for larger drums (bass drum, timpani, etc.) used at the college or professional level.

Obtaining the Correct Drum Sound

The correct drum sound depends on a number of factors the player must be aware of, including the style of music being played (such as marching, concert, rock or jazz) and how drum sounds are used in different settings. For example, concert and jazz style drumming will generally require a medium-thick head, while marching and rock style drumming will typically require a thick head.

4   How to Tune Your Drums

THE DRUM AND ITS PARTS

Many parts are common to all drums of a drumset. The snare drum is used here as a model for pointing out the various features. Parts specific to individual drums are addressed in the appropriate sections.

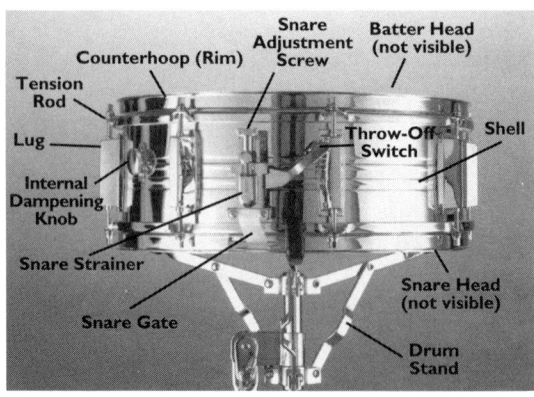

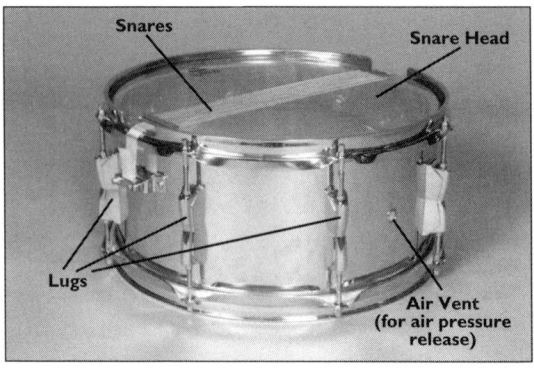

1. The top head of the snare drum is referred to as the *batter head*, and is available with either a smooth finish or rough, sand-like coating. The bottom head is called the *snare head*. As a general rule, the bottom head should be thinner and slightly tighter than the batter head. In most cases, the batter head will determine the timbre of the drum, but this, of course, will depend on the thickness, resonance and condition of the head.

2. The *flesh hoop* (originally a wooden piece around which damp calfskin was tucked) is a ring, usually metal, to which the head is attached by means of glue or pressure.

3. Drumheads are held in place by *counterhoops*, also referred to as *rims*. They are made of either metal or wood and sit on top of the flesh hoop, holding the head onto the rim with the help of *tension rods*.

4. The *shell* is the frame that supports all the other components of the drum. It may be constructed of wood, sometimes with a lacquer or pearl finish, or made of metal or fiberglass.

5. The *bearing edge* is the point on the snare drum where the head meets the rim. Usually cut at a 45-degree angle, this edge must evenly touch the drumhead to insure its proper seating on the shell.

6. *Lugs* are attached to the side of the drum shell and serve as receptacles for the tension rods.

7. *Tension rods* hold the counterhoop in place and are used to adjust the tension of the drumhead. The number of rods and lugs attached to the snare drum depends upon the size of the drum, but the usual number is 8 to 10 for most drums.

8. The *air vent* is a hole in the side of the drum shell that allows air to escape when the batter head is struck.

9. The *snare strainer*, also called the *snare release*, allows the snares to be engaged or disengaged from the snare head by means of a throw-off switch.

10. The *tension adjustment knob* is located on top of the throw-off switch. Turning it clockwise or counter-clockwise allows you to adjust the tension or pressure of the snares as they lie across the bottom head.

11. *Snares* are wire, gut or plastic strands that stretch across the outside surface of the bottom head.

    a. Gut snares are made of catgut. They produce a dark, crisp and articulate sound, but are lacking in the ability to respond at softer dynamic levels. Like calfskin heads, they can be affected by weather and are commonly used in the marching field.

b. Wire snares are made of coiled, spring-like strands. They have a bright sound and respond well at lower dynamic levels. As a result, they are the preferred choice of concert percussionists and drumset players.

c. Plastic (nylon) snares are brighter than gut snares and are not affected by weather. They are articulate, and effective for marching use.

12. The *tone control* or *internal dampening knob* is mounted on the outside of the shell and attached to an internal muffler. When the knob is turned clockwise, the muffler presses against the batter head to absorb some of the vibrations and eliminate the after-ring.

TUNING THE DRUMS

The most important aspect of drumset tuning is the balance that needs to exist between the components of the set. The determined pitch will depend largely on the style of music being played and the player's own personal taste. For example, rock styles most often employ a low, punchy tuning, whereas jazz styles tend to use mid- to high-pitched tunings. Tuning and muffling should be checked behind the drumset as well as from the vantagepoint of the audience. A fair amount of experimentation will be required to find what works best for you.

There are two methods for tuning drums: the *cross-tension system*, and the *clockwise system* of tensioning. The clockwise system of tensioning is the less useful of the two, as the head tends to wrinkle in undesirable places and does not sit properly on the bearing edge. This method of tuning is therefore inconsistent and undependable. By contrast, the cross-tension system maintains even tensioning around the drum throughout the entire tuning process.

The Snare Drum

Drumheads should be changed regularly. It is important to remember that the quality of sound continuously deteriorates as the drum is played; therefore, heads that are played loud and long (such as marching heads) will need to be changed more frequently than those played modestly and moderately (such as concert heads).

Changing the Drumhead

1. Determine the size of the drum by measuring from one side to the other, directly across the center. Do not include the hoop when measuring.
2. Select the proper replacement head, and check to make sure it is free from any defects, especially where the head enters the hoop.
3. Place the head, hoop down, onto a smooth countertop surface to see if it is straight.
4. Remove the tension rods, counterhoop and drumhead from your snare drum.
5. Clean the counterhoop and wipe the bearing edge of the shell clean. Wood and pearl finishes can be cleaned with a damp cloth and mild soap, and furniture polish may also be applied to wood finishes, if desired. Metal shells and hoops may be cleaned with a damp cloth and/or metal polish.
6. Before putting the new head in place, a thin coat of paraffin wax may be applied around the bearing edge of the drum shell (this is optional).
7. Set the new drumhead on the drum shell, and position it so the logo on the drumhead lines up with either the air hole or the drum shell logo.

8   How to Tune Your Drums

8. Place the counterhoop over the drumhead, and carefully replace the tension rods after lubricating them with Vaseline or light machine oil. Using your fingers, systematically screw each tension rod in place and tighten them using only slight finger pressure.

Before tuning, it will be helpful to number each tension rod using either the snare release, logo or air hole as a point of reference for tension rod number 1.

Tuning the Snare Drum
Using the Cross-Tension System

1. Tune the snare drum starting with the batter side. When incorporated into a drumset, the snare drum is usually tuned higher than the bass drum and tom-toms.

2. Starting with tension rod number 1, use a drum key or torque wrench (for marching drums) to tighten each rod one-half turn (or twist of the wrist). Do this repeatedly until the drumhead feels firm. Be sure not to tension any lug more than the others.

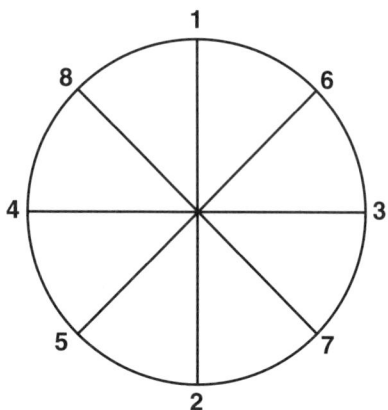

The Snare Drum 9

3. Once the initial tensioning of the drumhead is complete, you may get the head in tune with itself by *point tuning*. (Be sure to disengage the snares with the throw-off switch before beginning this step). Point tuning is achieved by tapping the head with a drumstick about two inches from each rod, to be certain the pitch is consistent all the way around the drum.

If it is not, adjust any location where the pitch is lower than average by turning the nearest tension rod clockwise as needed.

Adjust any location where the pitch is higher than average by turning the nearest tension rod counter-clockwise as needed.

Note: It is advisable to muffle the bottom head with something soft (like a pillow) while point tuning the top head, and vice versa. This will eliminate the problem of both heads resonating simultaneously, making it easier to point tune each individual head.

10   How to Tune Your Drums

4. The procedure for tuning the snare head is the same as for the batter head, but with one additional step. Before changing the head, remove the snares on the bottom side of the drum. (It is only necessary to disconnect the snares from one end of the drum).

5. Once the head has been replaced, reconnect the snares.

6. Tension the snare head firmly, but be sure that it is still able to vibrate freely against the snares. Some drummers tighten the batter head tighter than the snare, while others do the reverse. There is no firm rule; it is simply a matter of tone preference.

Tuning the Snare Drum
Using the Clockwise System

1. Starting with tension rod number 1, tighten each rod one twist of the wrist, moving sequentially around the drum in a circle.

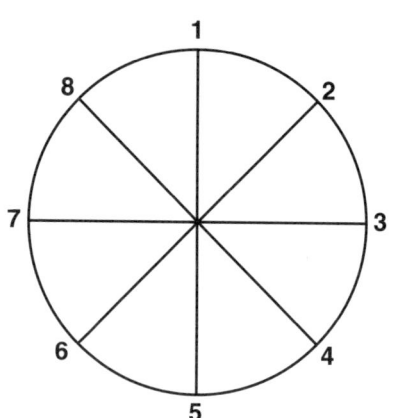

The Snare Drum **11**

2. Tap the head with a drumstick about two inches from each rod to be certain that the pitch is consistent all the way around the drum.

3. The procedure for tuning the snare head is the same as that for the batter head, but with one additional step. Before changing the head, remove the snares on the bottom side of the drum. (It is only necessary to disconnect the snares from one end of the drum).

4. Once the head has been replaced, reconnect the snares.

5. Tension the snare head firmly, but be sure that it is still able to vibrate freely against the snares. Some drummers tighten the batter head tighter than the snare, while others do the reverse. There is no firm rule; it is simply a matter of tone preference.

Setting the Head

1. Once the head is in place and the correct tension has been achieved, take the palm of your hand and place it in the center of the drumhead.

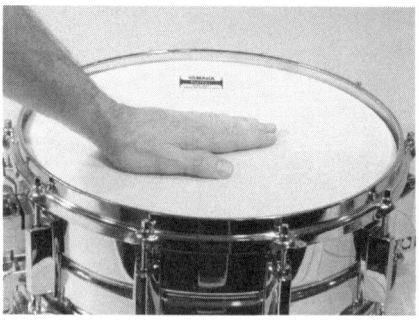

2. Place your other hand on top and press firmly on the head with both hands.

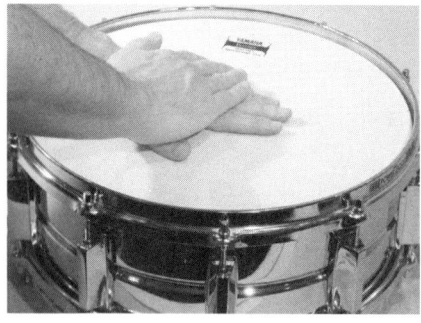

A cracking or popping sound is normal—it is simply the new head adjusting to the tension. Once this is done, the head will hold the tension consistently wherever you set it.

3. Make additional adjustments as needed.

Using the Snare Adjustment Screw

1. After achieving the desired pitch and tension for both heads, tap the batter head with a drumstick while adjusting the snare adjustment screw until the snares have been brought into contact with the snare head and the desired sound has been achieved.

The Bass Drum

2. Be careful not to over tighten the drumheads or the snares, as you will choke the drums sound. Remember that sound is produced by allowing the heads and snares to vibrate freely.

3. Test repeatedly by tapping the head lightly with a drumstick while making adjustments.

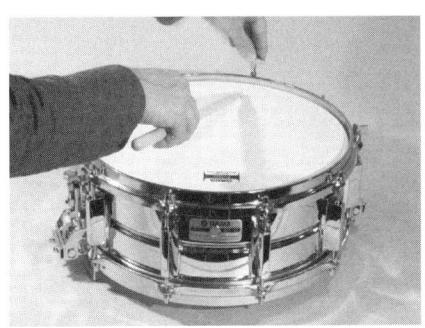

The Bass Drum

Drumset bass drum heads are referred to as the front head (audience side) and back head (player's side). Drumhead selection is made from a variety of combinations that may include coated, clear, pinstripe, black dot, etc. Again, head selection will be determined by the musical situation and the taste of the individual player.

front

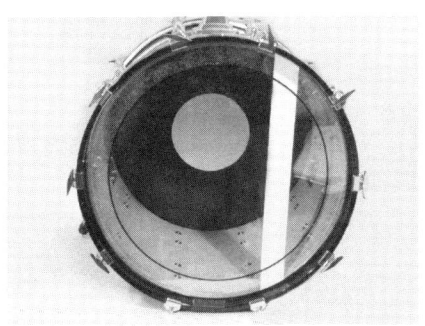

back

14 How to Tune Your Drums

Changing the Drumhead

1. Select the proper replacement head.

2. Remove the tension rods, counterhoop and drumhead from your bass drum.

3. Clean the counterhoop, and wipe the bearing edge of the shell clean. Wood and pearl finishes may be cleaned with a damp cloth and mild soap, and furniture polish may also be applied to wood finishes, if desired. Metal shells and hoops may be cleaned with a damp cloth and/or metal polish.

4. Before putting the new head in place, a thin coat of paraffin wax may be applied around the bearing edge of the drum shell (this is optional).

5. Set the new drumhead on the drum shell, and position it so the logo on the drumhead is at the top.

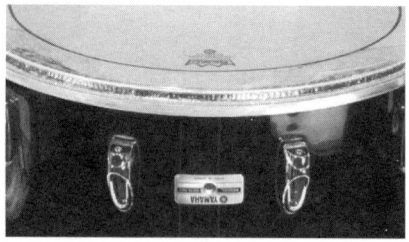

6. Place the counterhoop over the drumhead and carefully replace the tension rods after lubricating them with Vaseline or light machine oil. Using your fingers, screw each tension rod in place and tighten them using only slight finger pressure.

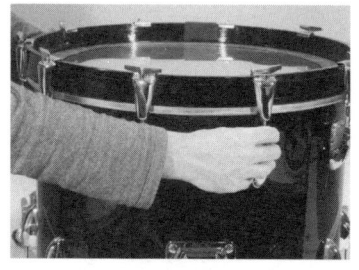

Before tuning, it will be helpful to number each tension rod using either the logo or air hole as a point of reference for tension rod number 1.

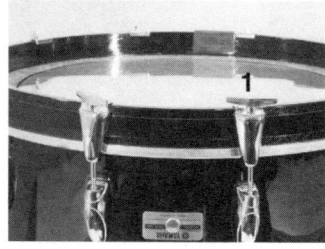

Tuning the Bass Drum
(Cross-Tension System)

A solid, front bass drum head that is tuned properly with the batter head can provide a huge, punchy sound. When the heads are tuned up in pitch (such as in a jazz idiom), a very musical, resonant sound can be produced, something that works well with smaller bass drums.

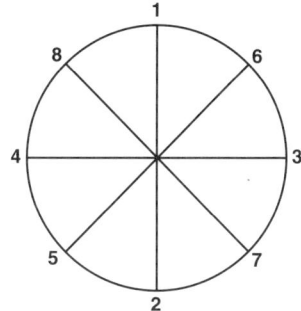

1. Tune the head by using the cross-tension system of tuning as described for the snare drum.

2. When tuning the bass drum, use your fingers to turn two opposite rods from the base until all are snug, then begin cross tensioning at the top, one-half turn each.

Continue this process until the desired pitch has been achieved. If the pitches are hard to hear, simply keep the amount of turns on each rod consistent. Higher tunings become more apparent.

3. Once the initial tensioning of the drumhead is complete, get the head in tune with itself by point tuning. This is achieved by tapping the head with a drumstick about two inches from each rod to be certain that the pitch is consistent all the way around the drum.

16   How to Tune Your Drums

If it is not, adjust any location where the pitch is lower than average by turning the nearest tension rod clockwise as needed.

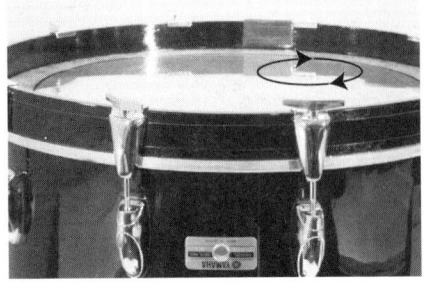

Adjust any location where the pitch is higher than average by turning the nearest tension rod counter-clockwise as needed.

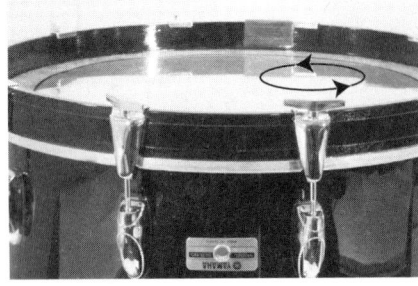

Note: It is advisable to muffle the bottom head with something soft (like a pillow) while point tuning the top head, and vice versa. This will eliminate the problem of both heads resonating simultaneously, making it easier to point tune each individual head.

Setting the Head

1. Once the head is in place and the correct tension has been applied, take the palm of your hand and place it in the center of the drumhead.

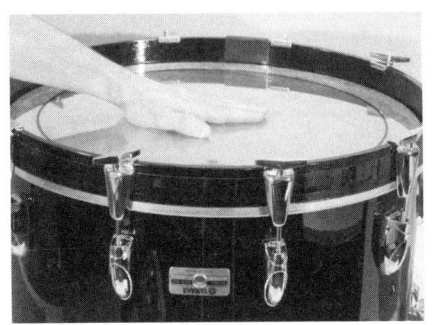

2. Place your other hand on top and press firmly on the head with both hands.

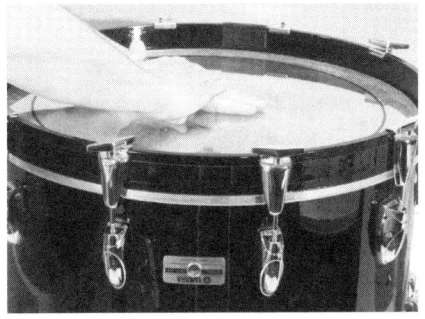

A cracking or popping sound is normal—it is simply the new head adjusting to the tension. Once this is done, the head will hold the tension consistently wherever you set it.

3. Make additional adjustments as needed.

The Tom-Toms

Both heads of the drumset toms are batter heads, and are simply referred to as the top and bottom heads. As with the bass drum, both heads of a single drum do not have to be the same type, and head selection will again be determined by the musical situation and the individual player's taste.

Changing the Drumhead

1. Select the proper replacement head.

2. Remove the tension rods, counterhoop and drumhead from your tom-tom.

3. Wipe the bearing edge of the shell clean. Wood and pearl finishes may be cleaned with a damp cloth and mild soap, and furniture polish may also be applied to wood finishes, if desired. Metal shells and hoops may be cleaned with a damp cloth and/or metal polish.

4. Before putting the new head in place, a thin coat of paraffin wax may be applied around the bearing edge of the drum shell (this is optional).

18 How to Tune Your Drums

5. Set the new drumhead on the drum shell and position it so the logo on the drumhead lines up with either the air hole or the drum shell logo.

6. Place the counterhoop over the drumhead and carefully replace the tension rods after lubricating them with Vaseline or light machine oil. Using your fingers, screw each tension rod in place and tighten them using only slight finger pressure.

Before tuning, it will be helpful to number each tension rod using either the logo or air hole as a point of reference for tension rod number 1.

The Tom-Toms

Tuning the Tom-Toms (Cross-Tension System)

1. Tune the head by using the cross-tension system of tuning as described for the snare drum.

2. It is important that the tension be equalized around the entire circumference of the tom-tom to obtain the best tone. Again, this is accomplished in much the same manner as for the snare drum.

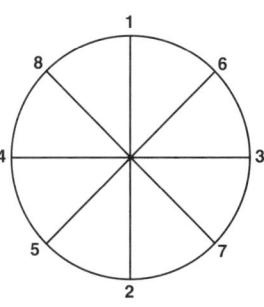

3. Once the initial tensioning of the drumhead is complete, get the head in tune with itself by point tuning. This is achieved by tapping the head with a drumstick about two inches from each rod to be certain that the pitch is consistent all the way around the drum.

If it is not, adjust any location where the pitch is lower than average by turning the nearest tension rod clockwise as needed.

Adjust any location where the pitch is higher than average by turning the nearest tension rod counter-clockwise as needed.

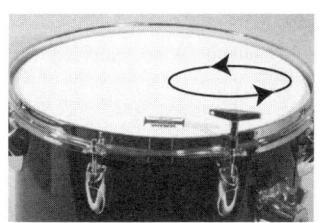

Note: It is advisable to muffle the bottom head with something soft (like a pillow) while point tuning the top head, and vice versa. This will eliminate the problem of both heads resonating simultaneously, making it easier to point tune each individual head.

Tuning Multiple Toms

Multiple tom-toms of varied diameters should be tuned from high to low as one moves from left to right. Some players prefer tuning the three tom-toms of a standard five-piece set using a triad (from low to high tom) with the bass drum tuned to a fourth below the low tom (also called the floor tom).

Setting the Head

1. Once the head is in place and the correct tension has been achieved, take the palm of your hand and place it in the center of the drumhead.

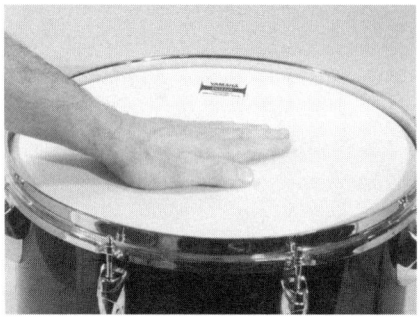

2. Place your other hand on top and press firmly on the head with both hands.

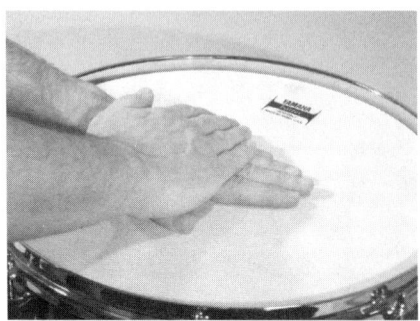

A cracking or popping sound is normal—it is simply the new head adjusting to the new tension. Once this is done, the head will hold the tension consistently wherever you set it.

3. Make additional adjustments as needed.

MUFFLING

In various musical or studio situations, a certain amount of ring or harmonic overtones may need to be removed from the sound. In order to reduce the desired amount of head resonance, drums can be muffled in a variety of ways, including placing tape, gauze, foam or other materials on the surface of the drumhead. It is important to remember that placing any material on the head will reduce the resonance and projection of drum.

Several drum companies manufacture effective muffling systems such as the Evans EQ Pad, the Remo Muffls and the DW Drum Pillow. Each of these systems will provide adequate and adjustable muffling.

Muffling the Snare Drum

1. The desired balance of dampening and resonance may be achieved by selecting the right type of head.

2. If more dampening is desired, additional muffling can be achieved by placing a small amount of duct tape or piece of cloth to the top exterior of the batter head, near the edge.

3. The use of the internal muffler included on some models is not recommended, as it muffles the head by applying pressure from the underside of the head, restricting the natural resonance of the drum.

Muffling the Tom-Toms

1. The desired balance of dampening and resonance may be achieved by selecting the right type of head.

2. If more dampening is desired, the tom-toms can be muffled by placing tape, gauze or

other materials on the surface of the head as needed to remove the desired amount of harmonics or ring from the sound.

Doing so, however, will reduce a certain amount of resonance, which may affect the projection of the drum.

Muffling the Bass Drum

1. The desired balance of dampening and resonance may be achieved by selecting the right type of head.

2. Felt strips may be placed behind both heads of the bass drum, and some players may choose to place a pillow, blanket or piece of foam rubber inside the drum. In this case, the cost is minimal, and the sound can be customized to fit your needs.

Keep in mind, however, that while this effectively muffles the drum, it also produces a sound that lacks resonance, making the timbre of this drum different than that of the other drums in the set.

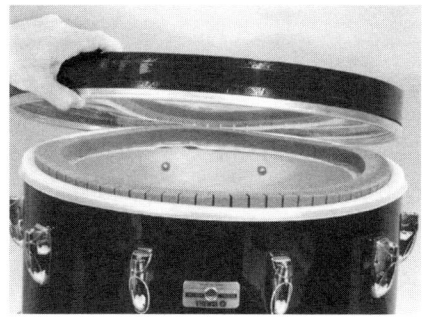

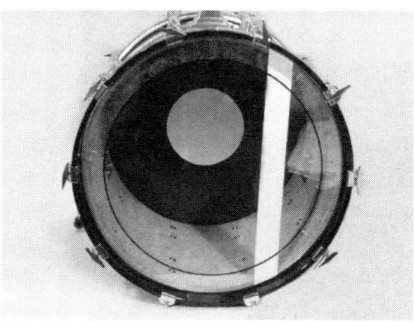

3. Front bass drum heads may also be purchased either with a six-inch hole cut off-center, or with a larger center hole. (If you would like to cut your own hole, the use of a hole-cutting template will allow you to choose your own placement.) The front hole allows air to escape, resulting in a more direct sound while retaining some of the resonant qualities of the front head. It also allows a microphone to be placed inside the drum at varying degrees.

24 How to Tune Your Drums